Maggie

It's all about...

SUPER SOLAR SYSTEM

KINGFISHER

First published 2015 by Kingfisher
an imprint of Pan Macmillan
20 New Wharf Road, London N1 9RR
Associated companies throughout the world
www.panmacmillan.com

Series editor: Sarah Snashall
Series design: Little Red Ant
Adapted from an original text by Hannah Wilson

ISBN 978-0-7534-3892-3

9 8 7 6 5 4 3 2 1

1SP/1215/MPA/UG/128MA

A CIP catalogue record for this book is available from the British Library.

Printed in China

Picture credits
The Publisher would like to thank the following for permission to reproduce their material.
Top = t; Bottom = b; Centre = c; Left = l; Right = r
Cover Shutterstock/Vadim Sadovski; Back cover NASA; Pages 2–3, 30–31 Shutterstock/
Traveller Martin; 4 Shutterstock/PaulPaladin; 5 Shutterstock/Dudarev Mikhail;
6–7 Kingfisher Artbank; 8–9 Shutterstock/USBFCO; 9 Kingfisher Artbank; 10 Shutterstock/
MarcelClemens; 11 Shutterstock/GK; 12–13 Shutterstock/PavleMarjanovic; 12 Shutterstock/
Lilkar; 14–15 NASA; 16–17 Shutterstock/Traveller Martin; 17 NASA/JPL; 18–19 NASA/JPL-
Caltech/MSSS; 18 NASA/Hubble Heritage Team (STScI/AURA); 20 Shutterstock/Kirschner;
21–22 Shutterstock/MarcelClemens; 23 Shutterstock/Shalygin; 23b NASA; 24 Shutterstock/
EpicStockMedia; 25t NASA/JPL-Caltech; 25b NASA/ESA/Caltech; 26t NASA/EIT/SOHO/ESA;
26c NASA/Hubble Heritage Team (STScI/AURA); 26b NASA/Walt Feimer; 27 Kingfisher
Artbank; 28 Shutterstock/Prometheus72; 29 NASA/STScI; 29b NASA/ESA/Hubble Heritage
Team (STScI/AURA); 32 Shutterstock/John A Davis.
Cards: Front bl Shutterstock/Vadim Sadovski; Back bl Shutterstock/Jaan-Martin Kuusmann;
all other images Kingfisher Artbank.

Front cover: A photorealistic illustration of stars and planets.

CONTENTS

For your free audio download go to
http://panmacmillan.com/SuperSolarSystem
or goo.gl/RXDiS2
Happy listening!

Starry night

Look up at the sky at night. Can you see the Moon? It is a huge ball of rock that travels round the Earth. Can you see any stars? Each star is a giant ball of hot, glowing gas further away than you can imagine.

Our closest star is the Sun!

FACT...

Our galaxy may contain 500 thousand million stars.

The Solar System

The Sun is so large that it pulls planets towards it. The Earth and seven other planets travel round the Sun. The Sun and these planets make up our Solar System.

Uranus

Jupiter

Mars

SPOTLIGHT: The Sun

Size compared to Earth:	1.3 million times bigger
Distance from Earth:	150 million km
Made from:	hot gas
Fact:	4.6 billion years old

Neptune

Sun

Mercury

Venus

Earth

Saturn

7

You must never look directly at the Sun. Its very strong light can damage your eyes.

Night and day

The Earth spins on an imaginary stick called an axis. Imagine a pencil stuck through the middle of a spinning orange.

Day happens when one side of the Earth faces the Sun. Night happens when the same side faces away. It takes 24 hours for the Earth to spin all the way round once.

The Earth takes one year to travel round the Sun. As it moves, different parts of the Earth are closer to the Sun. This movement causes the seasons.

FACT...

As the Earth spins round, it is daytime in places that face the Sun. But 12 hours later, the same places face away from the Sun and it is nighttime.

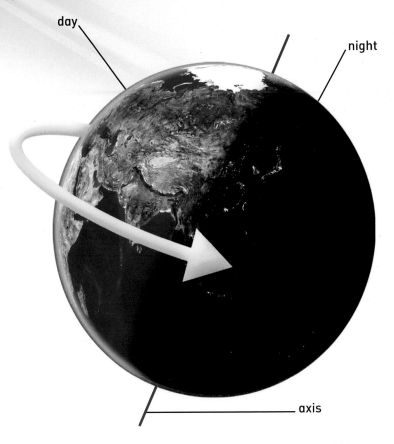

day

night

axis

The Moon

A moon is a ball of rock that travels round a planet. Our Moon is a dry, rocky place with no wind or rain. Nothing can live there.

The Moon orbits the Earth.

Look closely at the Moon on a clear night. The dark patches you see are huge flat plains. The light patches are mountains and the rings are craters.

SPOTLIGHT: The Moon

Size compared to Earth: one-seventh of the size
Distance from Earth: 384,400 km
Made from: rock
Fact: orbits Earth in 28 days

The changing Moon

The Moon shines at night because light from the Sun bounces off its surface. As the Moon travels round the Earth, different parts of the Moon face the Sun and shine.

When the Moon is full, it is facing the Sun.

In the 28 days it takes for the Moon to travel round the Earth, the Moon changes from a full circle to a thin curve to nothing and back again.

FACT...

As the Moon travels round the Earth it spins slowly, always keeping the same side facing us.

full moon

crescent moon

Moon landings

On 20 July, 1969 American astronauts Neil Armstrong and Buzz Aldrin became the first people to stand on the Moon.

They travelled across the Moon's surface in a moon buggy and collected rock samples. A total of 12 men have walked on the Moon so far.

A huge rocket blasted the lunar spacecraft into space. It took three days to reach the Moon.

Footprints left on the Moon by the astronauts will last for millions of years because there is no wind or rain to remove them!

Astronauts' bodies are lighter on the Moon so the astronauts bounce when they walk.

Star or planet?

The brightest star in the sky is not a star at all! It looks like a star but it doesn't twinkle. It is Venus, our closest planet and probably the harshest place in the whole Solar System.

Moon

You can often see Venus in the sky just after sunset.

SPOTLIGHT: Venus

Size compared to Earth: almost the same size

Distance from Earth: 5.5 million km²

Made from: rock

Fact: hottest planet

The surface of Venus is covered with volcanoes and craters.

The Red Planet

Mars is a rocky planet covered with red soil. It is home to Olympus Mons, the largest volcano in the Solar System.

Astronauts hope to travel to Mars this century.

SPOTLIGHT: Mars

Size compared to Earth:	about half the size
Distance from Earth:	56 million km at closest
Made from:	rocks, soil and ice
Fact:	called the Red Planet

Robots have been sent to Mars to investigate the planet and to look for signs of life, such as fossils.

The Mars rover took photographs of Mars and examined the soil.

Gassy giants

Jupiter and Saturn, the two biggest planets in the Solar System, are giant balls of gas and liquid. Jupiter has 67 moons, and storms swirl round its outer layers creating beautiful patterns.

The Earth could easily fit inside Jupiter's Great Red Spot.

FACT...

A hurricane on Jupiter, called the Great Red Spot, has been raging for at least 300 years.

Saturn is the easiest planet to recognize. Lumps of ice and dust spin round this planet, creating rings round its equator.

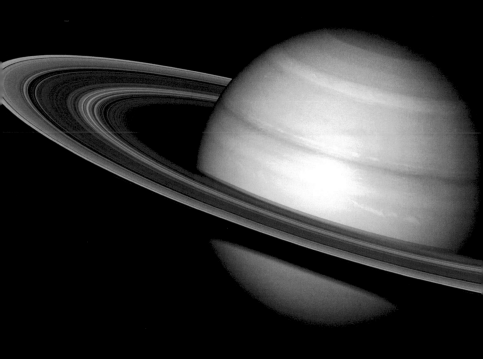

Saturn has 7 rings and 62 moons.

Comets and shooting stars

A comet is a bright lump of ice with a glowing tail. A bright comet is rarely seen in the skies above the Earth.

The comet Hale-Bopp was last seen above the Earth on 1 April, 1997.

When a lump of space rock enters the
Earth's atmosphere it causes a streak
of light in the sky. This is called a
shooting star,
or meteor.

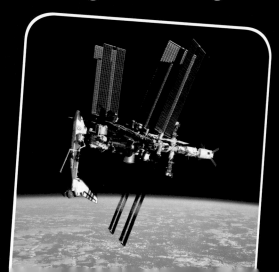

The International
Space Station looks
like a moving star as
it crosses the sky.

Galaxies far, far away

If you look up into the sky on a clear night, you might see a milky-white cloud of stars. This is the Milky Way galaxy – our galaxy. A galaxy is a group of stars. Our Sun is just one of billions of stars in the Milky Way.

You have to be far from bright city lights on a clear night to see the Milky Way.

Scientists think our galaxy, the
Milky Way, looks like this.

our Sun

The Universe is made up of countless
galaxies stretching out as far as you
can imagine.

Each speck of light in this view of deep
space is a different galaxy.

Colours and patterns

The Sun looks yellow or orange, but other stars can be different colours. There are red giants, red dwarfs and blue giants.

Stars are formed inside clouds called nebulas.

Blue giants are a thousand times larger than the Sun, and much hotter.

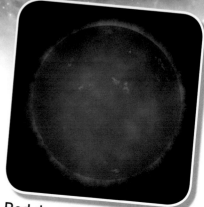

Red dwarfs are smaller and cooler than our Sun.

People have always loved to make up patterns, called constellations, out of the stars. Imagine drawing lines to join up the stars and form a picture.

Can you find Hercules and Pegasus on this map of the constellations?

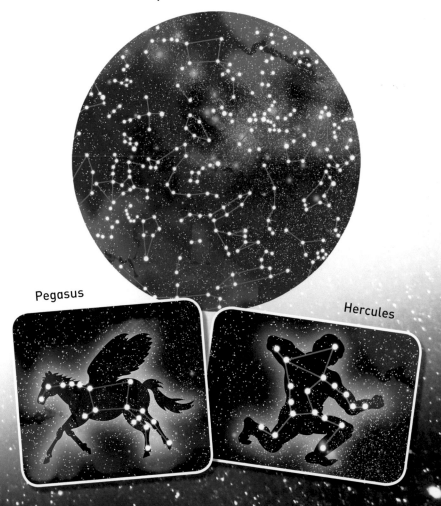

Pegasus

Hercules

Star gazing

If you look at the night sky with the naked eye, you can see stars and planets. If you look with binoculars you can see the moons of Jupiter. If you use a telescope you can see the rings of Saturn.

Scientists use huge telescopes far from city lights to see distant galaxies and comets.

The Hubble Space Telescope orbits the Earth and has been taking photographs of deep space for more than 25 years!

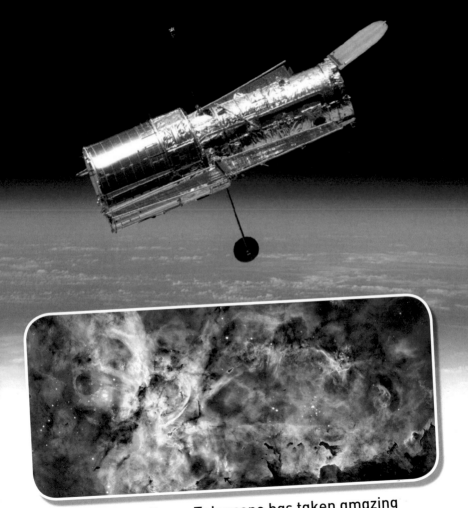

The Hubble Space Telescope has taken amazing pictures of the Universe.

GLOSSARY

astronaut A person who travels into space.

atmosphere The layer of gas round a planet.

comet A lump of rock and ice that travels round the Sun.

crater A dent left in a planet or moon by an impact from a giant rock.

equator An imaginary line round the middle of a planet.

fossil The solid rocky remains of an animal or plant that lived long ago.

galaxy A group of millions of stars, planets, gas and dust that spin together in space.

gas A substance that is not a solid or a liquid.

hurricane A violent spinning wind storm.

lunar To do with the Moon.

Mars rover A robot vehicle that went to Mars and travelled across the planet's surface.

meteor A shooting star caused by a space rock burning up in the Earth's atmosphere.

moon A large rocky sphere that travels round a planet.

moon buggy A small vehicle that travelled across the Moon's surface.

nebula A cloud of dust and gas.

orbit To travel round the Sun or a planet.

planet A large, ball-shaped object that travels round a star in space.

season A time of year with certain weather patterns.

telescope An instrument that shows faraway objects more clearly.

INDEX